CHRISTIAN JOURNAL WRITING PRIMARY

Introduction

Christian Journal Writing Primary has been designed to provide children with daily journal activities that reinforce Christian values and virtues. The book is divided into 12 themes which feature writing activities relating to each of the following virtues and values: kindness, fairness, faith, responsibility, friendship, love, honesty, loyalty, trust, courage, hope, and family fun.

Each theme can be used on a monthly basis if desired, and there are enough activities presented for children to practice writing every day. These activities are a lot of fun for children to complete and include writing poems, making cards, creating songs, composing prayers, reading and writing Bible verses, and much more. Also included throughout the book are craft ideas and games that help children further understand the importance of the values and virtues presented. Some activities will be able to be done easily by the children. Others may need to be explained. Read each activity in advance and be prepared to help and guide the children when necessary.

Page 32 contains a nice border that can be used in a variety of ways. Let children draw pictures or write about special times relating to the themes. Or, use it to write notes to others, to create awards, or to start prayers or poems the children finish. Be creative!

This book is a perfect way for children to have a lot of fun as they learn about important Christian virtues and values and improve their writing skills at the same time.

Written by Kathy Zaun
Illustrated by Mark Mason

Scripture taken from the HOLY BIBLE, NEW INTERNATIONAL VERSION. Copyright © 1973, 1978, 1984 by International Bible Society. Used by permission of Zondervan Publishing House.

GP-75505 Christian Journal Writing Primary
All rights reserved—Printed in the U.S.A.
Copyright © 1997 Grace Publications
23740 Hawthorne Blvd., Torrance, CA 90505

Kindness

> "... that I am the Lord, who exercises kindness ..."
>
> *Jeremiah 9:24*

SUNDAY	MONDAY	TUESDAY	WEDNESDAY	THURSDAY	FRIDAY	SATURDAY
Write the name of someone who is kind.	Write three ways you have been kind today.	Write three words that rhyme with kind.	Draw a picture of you being kind.	Read Matthew 7:12. This is the Golden Rule. Write it and memorize it.	Draw a picture of you following the Golden Rule.	Make a collage of pictures showing kindness.
List three ways you are kind.	Create a kindness poster.	Read a book about someone who is kind.	Write a prayer asking God to help you be kind.	Draw a picture of someone being unkind.	Finish this sentence: *I like to be kind because* ___	List three ways God is kind to you.
Write a song about being kind.	Find pictures of everyone to whom you are kind.	Cut out a picture showing kindness. Write about it.	Make a card for a kind person.	Write the name of the kindest person you know.	Draw a picture of someone being kind.	Find kind in a dictionary. Write the definition of it.
List three ways you are kind to your family.	List three ways you are kind to your friends.	Write *kind*. Glue pictures around the word.	Make a thank-you card for someone who has been kind to you.	Kindness is a virtue. Write another virtue.	Write one way your parents are kind to you.	Finish this sentence: *I am kind when I* ___
		Write another word for *kind*.	Write a sentence with the word *kind* in it.			Write a prayer asking God to help someone you know be kind.

Let's Have Fun!

It is easy to have fun when people are kind to each other. Some people below are not being kind. Put an X on the people who are not showing God's love. Color the people who are being kind.

    GP-75505 Journal Writing Primary

A Kindness Card

God wants us to be kind to each other. Thank someone for being kind.

Cut out the card below. Color the front and back covers (1, 4). Write a note thanking someone for being kind on side 3. Draw a special picture on side 2. Fold on the dotted lines. Give the card to a friend.

1

Thank you for being KIND!

4

You are very SPECIAL!

Fold on this line first.

2

Dear __________,

____

____

____

____

____

Love,

____

3

Fairness

If a king judges the poor with fairness, his throne will always be secure.
Proverbs 29:14

SUNDAY	MONDAY	TUESDAY	WEDNESDAY	THURSDAY	FRIDAY	SATURDAY
	Create a card thanking someone for being fair.	Finish this sentence: *I think _____ is fair because _______.*	Draw a picture of you being fair.	Create an award to give to a fair person.	Cut out a picture showing fairness. Write about it.	Create a fairness poster.
Write one way you were fair.	Draw a picture of your parents being fair to you.	List three ways your teacher is fair.	Write a prayer asking God to help you be fair.	Draw a picture of three words that rhyme with fair.	Write one way God is fair.	
Write *fairness.* Cut out and glue pictures showing fairness around the word.	Write a sentence with the word *fair* in it.	Make a list of community workers who are fair.	Write the names of three people who you think are fair.		Finish this sentence: *It wasn't fair when _____________.*	Write why it is important to be fair.
Read a book about someone who is fair.	Write a story about something unfair.		Draw a picture of something unfair that happened to you.	Write a prayer asking God to help someone be fair.	Make up a rap song about fairness.	Write a poem about being fair. Include the words *bear* and *care* in it.
Fairness is a virtue. Write another virtue.	Write about a time when you were not fair.	Write 10 words relating to fairness. Alphabetize them.	Use the word *fairness* in a sentence.		Find fair in a dictionary. Write the definition of it.	Write the name of the fairest person you know.

5

That's Not Fair!

Fairness is a very important virtue. Everyone wants to be treated fairly.

Below are situation cards about fairness. Cut them out and put them in a stack. Sit down with your family or friends and take turns choosing cards. Let the person who chose the card tell what he or she would do in that situation. Then discuss the situation as a group.

It was Jody's turn to be first in line. Sam ran up and said he was first because it was his birthday. The coach let Sam go first. Was this fair?	Maria's mom said she could not have two cookies. Dinner was almost ready. Maria's sister took three cookies. Was this fair?
Jamie bought a book for $5. He didn't see the sign that said, "Buy One, Get One Free." He asked the clerk if he could get another book. She said, "Too bad. You lose!" Was this fair?	Tori, Tara, and Tim were taking turns on two swings. Brad wanted to swing, too. The three friends told Brad that they weren't done swinging, and he would have to find something else to do. Was this fair?
Brittney and Shelby had new pink pencil cases. Shelby lost hers. She told their mom that Brittney took hers. The girls' mom got mad at Brittney. Was this fair?	Mrs. Smith and Mrs. Jones were shopping. Mrs. Smith was looking for blue towels. Mrs. Jones found four blue towels but decided to buy them for herself. Was this fair?
Mrs. Tucker gave Lindsay some cookies to share with her friends. Lindsay shared them with her three best friends but wouldn't give cookies to anyone else. Was this fair?	Brendon and Scott were taking turns on the computer. Each boy got five minutes to play. Brendon couldn't tell time, so Scott kept giving himself seven minutes to play. Was this fair?

Faith

"... Have faith in the Lord your God and you will be upheld ..."

2 Chronicles 20:20

SUNDAY	MONDAY	TUESDAY	WEDNESDAY	THURSDAY	FRIDAY	SATURDAY
Write a definition of faith.	Read a story about faith. Write about it.	Draw a picture of you showing faith.	Finish this sentence: *I showed faith when* ___________.	Write a prayer asking God for faith.	Draw a picture of you being faithful.	Write the names of three people to whom you are faithful.
Draw a picture of Jesus being faithful.		Write about something your family can do to show their faith.	Draw a picture of you being unfaithful.	Write why it is important for you to be faithful.	Read Luke 17:19. Write if you wish faith could heal.	Use crayons to write the word *faith* all over a sheet of paper.
List three people who are faithful.	Write about a little boy who has faith.	Draw a picture of a little girl who has no faith.		Make up a song about faith.	Write why your faith is strong.	Write a poem about faith.
	Read Luke 18:8. Do you think a lot of people have faith?	Draw pictures showing things your faith helps you do.	Draw a picture of your family showing faith.	Find a picture that shows faith. Write about it.	Make a book of faith pictures.	Create an award for someone who has great faith.
Write three other Bible words that have the long a sound like *faith*.	List three people who have faith in you.	Write about a time when you needed faith.	Make a card for someone who has great faith.	Finish this sentence: *Faith is* ___________.		Using each letter in the word *faith*, write a word that begins with each letter.

GP-75505 Journal Writing Primary

Faithful Fun

Let everyone know that you are faithful to God! Decorate the banner below. Draw pictures on it that show how you are faithful. Cut it out. Fold on the dotted line. Get a piece of string about 30" long. Lay the middle part of the string on the fold. Glue the folded edge of the paper down over the string. Tie the ends. Hang and enjoy!

GP-75505 Journal Writing Primary

Responsibility

Brothers, each man, as responsible to God, should remain in the situation God called him to.

1 Corinthians 7:24

SUNDAY	MONDAY	TUESDAY	WEDNESDAY	THURSDAY	FRIDAY	SATURDAY
Write what responsibility is.	Draw a picture of you being responsible at home.	List three responsibilities you have at home.	Make a collage of pictures of people being responsible.	Draw a picture of Jesus being responsible.	Create an award to give to a responsible person.	Draw a picture of your family being responsible.
Write why it is important to be responsible.	Finish this sentence: *I am responsible when* _____________.		Design a card thanking someone for being responsible.	Write the word *responsible.* Glue pictures around it showing responsibility.	Write how you are responsible at home.	Draw a picture of someone you know who is responsible.
Draw a picture of you being responsible at church.	List five responsibilities your parents have.	Read a story about someone who is responsible. Write about it.	Write about a little girl who wasn't responsible.		Cut out a picture showing responsibility. Glue it to paper and give it a title.	Make a poster telling others to be responsible.
Write a prayer. Ask God to help you be responsible.	Draw a flower. Write a responsibility you have in each petal.		Draw a picture of you being responsible at church.	Write a story that begins: *I wish I had been more responsible.*	Finish this sentence: _____ *isn't very responsible because* _____.	Find a picture of someone famous who has many responsibilities.
Write three responsibilities you have to animals.	Write a responsibility you wish you didn't have.	List three responsibilities Jesus had as God's son.	Make four words using the letters in *responsibility.*	God wants us to take care of the earth. List three ways to do this.		Write a song about responsibility.

Serious About Responsibility

God wants us all to work together. Everyone has certain responsibilities. These responsibilities include many chores. Sit down with your family or friends and decide what chores need to be done. Write each one on a strip of paper. Then cut out and color the scenes below. Glue the scenes to a paper sack. You have created a "Super Sack 'O Responsibility." Every day each person should choose one chore to do.

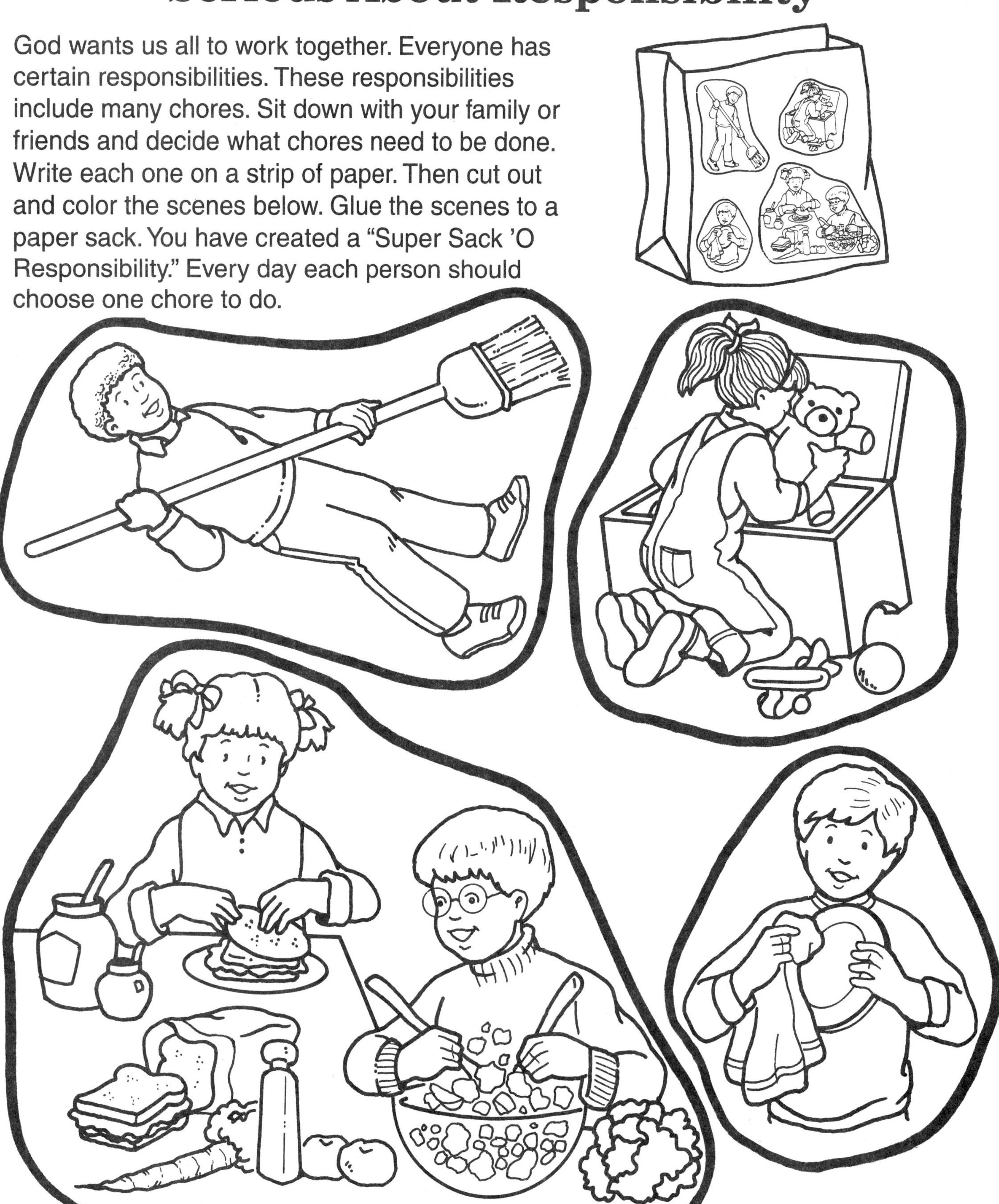

Reward Yourself!

God wants us to be responsible. Below is a chart to help you learn to be a responsible person. Fill in four chores that need to be done each day. Keep track of when you do each one. When you show that you can be responsible for a whole week straight, reward yourself with one of the rewards below.

Chore	Mon.	Tues.	Wed.	Thurs.	Fri.	Sat.	Sun.
1.							
2.							
3.							
4.							

GP-75505 Journal Writing Primary

Friendship

A friend loves at all times . . .
Proverbs 17:17

SUNDAY	MONDAY	TUESDAY	WEDNESDAY	THURSDAY	FRIDAY	SATURDAY
Draw a picture of you and your friends.	Write what friendship means to you.	Make a card for a special friend.		Cut out a picture of friends. Write why it is good to have friends.	Write the word *friends*. Draw pictures of your friends around it.	Write three things friends do.
	Draw a picture of your best friend.	Write three things friends don't do.	Write a prayer asking God to bless your friends.	Create an award to give a friend who did something special.	Read John 15:13. Write about it.	Make a list of all your friends.
Write a poem about friends. Include these words: *fun, sun,* and *God.*	Write how God is your friend.	Find a book about friends. Read it. Write the title of it.	Finish this sentence: *A friend is someone who _________.*	Write why it is important to have friends.		Draw a picture of you doing something nice for a friend.
Read John 15:14. Write why this wouldn't work for you.	Draw a picture of your best friend at church.		Create a song about friends.	Write a story that begins: *The best friend I ever had . . .*	Cut out pictures of things friends do. Glue them to a sheet of paper.	Write a poem for a special friend.
Draw something you would like to give your best friend.	Read Proverbs 16:28. Write if you agree with this.	Write three things you love about your best friend.	Write how you are a good friend.		Write three words that rhyme with friend.	Draw a picture of your best friend at school.

Friendly Fun

God gave us friends to enjoy. Good friends can have a lot of fun together. Create a "Friendly Fun" necklace. To do this, simply follow the directions below.

1. Cut out the necklace pattern.
2. Trace around it several times on tagboard.
3. Draw or paste a picture of friends having fun together on each pattern.
4. Punch a hole in each pattern piece as shown.
5. Cut a piece of string or yarn about 18" long.
6. Thread the string through the pictures.
7. Tie the ends together.
8. Wear and enjoy.

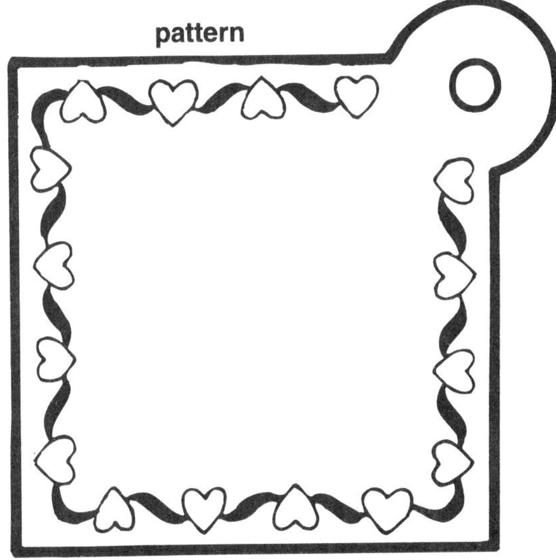

The Golden Rule

"So in everything, do to others what you would have them do to you . . ." *Matthew 7:12*

Being a good friend is very important. Good friends have a lot of fun together. Write a letter to a friend below. Thank your friend for being a good friend. Give the letter to your friend.

     GP-75505 Journal Writing Primary

Friendship Frame

God wants us all to have friends. Friends are very special people. Decorate the frame below. Fill in the lines to create a poem about one of your friends. Then draw or glue a picture of you and your friend in the empty space. Cut out the frame and give it to your special friend.

Love

Love the Lord your God with all your heart and with all your soul and with all your strength.

Deuteronomy 6:5

SUNDAY	MONDAY	TUESDAY	WEDNESDAY	THURSDAY	FRIDAY	SATURDAY
Write what love means to you.	List all the people who love you.	List all the people you love.	Draw a picture of the people whom you love most.	Make a special card telling someone how much you love him or her.		Write the word *love*. Cut out and glue pictures around it showing love.
Write a poem about love. Include these words: *love* and *above*.		Draw a picture of something you love.	Finish this sentence: *I love it when__________.*	Write three reasons why God loves you.	Draw a heart. Write the word *love* all around it.	Write the title of a book about love.
Find the word *love* in the Bible. Write the sentence.	Write three reasons why you love your parents.	Cut out a picture showing love. Write about it.	Create a song about love.	Write a song you know about love.		Write why it is important to love others.
Draw a picture of how you would feel if no one loved anyone.	Write three reasons why your parents love you.	Cut out a picture of someone who needs love. Write about it.	Finish this sentence: *God loves __________.*	Write what you would tell a baby about love.	Write what the world would be like if everyone loved everyone.	Write one way you can share God's love.
Draw a picture of you sharing God's love.	Write how much you love God.		Read the story of Daniel. (Daniel 6) Write how he loved God.	God says, "Love your enemies." Write why you think he says this.	Read John 13:34. Write if you obey this command.	Write the opposite of love.

Connected by Love

God wants us all to love one another. Families are people who love us a lot. Cut out the pattern below. Trace around it as many times as you need until you have one for each member of your family. Decorate each one to look like a person in your family. Glue the "hands" of each pattern together to create your family "connected by love."

Gifts of Love

God has given us many gifts. Plants, animals, friends, food, nature, family—all of these are gifts. Cut out the gift box below. Make a slit in it on the dotted line. Then decorate the gift box. Have someone fold and staple the sides and top together. Cut out or draw small pictures of all the gifts God has given you. Put them in the "box." Share your gifts with others.

Fold.

Honesty

. . . because they acted with complete honesty.
2 Kings 12:15

SUNDAY	MONDAY	TUESDAY	WEDNESDAY	THURSDAY	FRIDAY	SATURDAY
Draw a picture of you being honest.	Create a card for someone who is honest.	Draw a picture of a famous honest person.	Finish this sentence: *It is important to be honest because* ___________.	Write the definition of honesty.	Write the word *honest.* Cut out and glue pictures that show honesty around it.	Draw a picture of someone being dishonest.
Write three reasons why it is important to be honest.	Write a story about a dishonest person.	Read Proverbs 12:17. Write another proverb about honesty.		Create a song about honesty.	The *h* is silent in honesty. Write another word in which the *h* is silent.	Write what happens to people who are not honest.
Using crayons, write the word *honesty* all over a sheet of paper.		Write a prayer asking God to help others be honest.	List all the honest people you know.	Write words that begin with each letter in *honest.*	Design a poster telling others to be honest.	Write about a time when you were honest.
Write about a time when you were dishonest.	Find a story about a dishonest person. Write about it.	Write a poem about honesty. Include the words *true* and *do.*		Finish this sentence: _______ *wasn't* honest when ___________.	Read a book about honesty. Write the title.	Write a letter telling a friend how to be honest.
	Write why Jesus wants us to be honest.	"Honesty is the best policy." Write if you agree with this.	List three things dishonest people do.	List three things honest people do.	Draw a picture of a happy, honest person.	Write why you think some people are honest and some people aren't.

Honesty Is the Best Policy!

It is important to be honest. See how honest you are by playing the game below. Color the gameboard. Cut it out. Glue it onto a piece of posterboard. Get a marker for each player and a die. Take turns rolling the die and moving the number of spaces rolled. Do what is asked in the space you land on. The first person to finish is the most honest winner!

Loyalty

> "O Lord, God of our fathers Abraham, Isaac and Israel, keep this desire in the hearts of your people forever, and keep their hearts loyal to you."
>
> *1 Chronicles 29:18*

SUNDAY	MONDAY	TUESDAY	WEDNESDAY	THURSDAY	FRIDAY	SATURDAY
Read Ruth 1:16. Write how Ruth was loyal.	Write what loyalty is.		Noah was loyal to God. Draw a picture of Noah's ark.	God loved Noah. Draw a picture of God and Noah.	Write to whom you are loyal.	Draw a picture of you not being loyal to God.
Make a card to give to a loyal friend.	Finish this sentence: I am loyal to ____ when ____.	Write about a time when you weren't loyal.	Create an award to give to a loyal friend.		List who is loyal to you.	Write why being loyal is important.
Read a story about loyalty. Write the title.	Cut out a picture showing loyalty. Write about it.	Make up a song about loyalty.	List three ways your family is loyal to God.	Write a word that rhymes with *loyal*.	Write a prayer asking God to keep you loyal to him.	Write the word *loyal*. Cut out pictures and glue them around the word.
Draw a picture of you being loyal to God.		Draw a picture of a loyal animal.	Finish this sentence: I *wasn't loyal to* ____ *when I* ____.	Write why God wants you to be loyal to him.	List three friends who are loyal to you.	Write how you show loyalty to your family.
Write a story about a little girl who was loyal.	Make a poster. Tell others to be loyal.	Write about what happened to Adam and Eve when they weren't loyal to God.		Write how you show loyalty to God.	Draw a picture of an animal you are or would want to be loyal to.	Write what you would tell someone about being loyal to God.

Noah Was Loyal

Long ago, God could only find one good man. His name was Noah. Noah was loyal to God. God saved Noah and his family from a flood.

Read the story of Noah. Cut out the ark below. Decorate it. Then trace around it on sheets of paper as many times as you need to write about the story of Noah. Cut out the shapes. Write one sentence on each shape. Draw a picture on each shape. Staple the shapes together to create a book.

Trust

Trust in the Lord and do good . . .
Psalm 37:3

SUNDAY	MONDAY	TUESDAY	WEDNESDAY	THURSDAY	FRIDAY	SATURDAY
Write what trust means to you.	Draw a picture of the people you trust the most.	List five people who trust you.	Write why it is important to trust people.	Write something for which you trust in God.	Create a card for someone you trust.	Design a bumper sticker. Write *Trust in God* on it.
Write two words that rhyme with trust.	Write about a time when someone didn't trust you.	Write the word *trust*. Draw pictures of people you trust around it.		Create a song about trust.	List five people your parents trust to help you.	Draw a picture of something you are trusted to do.
Read a book about trust. Write about it.		Cut out a picture showing trust. Write about it.	God trusted Noah. Write how you know this.	Write what God trusts you to do.	List three things you trust God to do.	Draw a picture of you being trusted.
Write a poem about trust. Include the words *must* and *trust*.	Finish this sentence: *I trust in God because* ________.	Write a story about a little boy who couldn't be trusted.	Draw a picture of you when you are not trusted.		Create a collage of pictures showing trust.	Create a poster telling others to trust in God.
Finish this sentence: *God trusts me because* ________.	Write how you would feel if someone trusted you.	Write one thing you trust your teacher to do.	Draw a picture of something you trust your parents to do.	Draw a picture of something you trust God to do.	Trust is a virtue. Write another virtue.	

GP-75505 Journal Writing Primary

Trust in the Lord

It is good to trust in God. He helps people who trust in him. Who do you trust besides God? Perhaps you trust your parents and your friends. Who trusts you? Your parents trust you to obey them. Perhaps a family pet trusts you to feed it. Finish the sentence below. Then draw pictures of people you trust and people who trust you in the windows below.

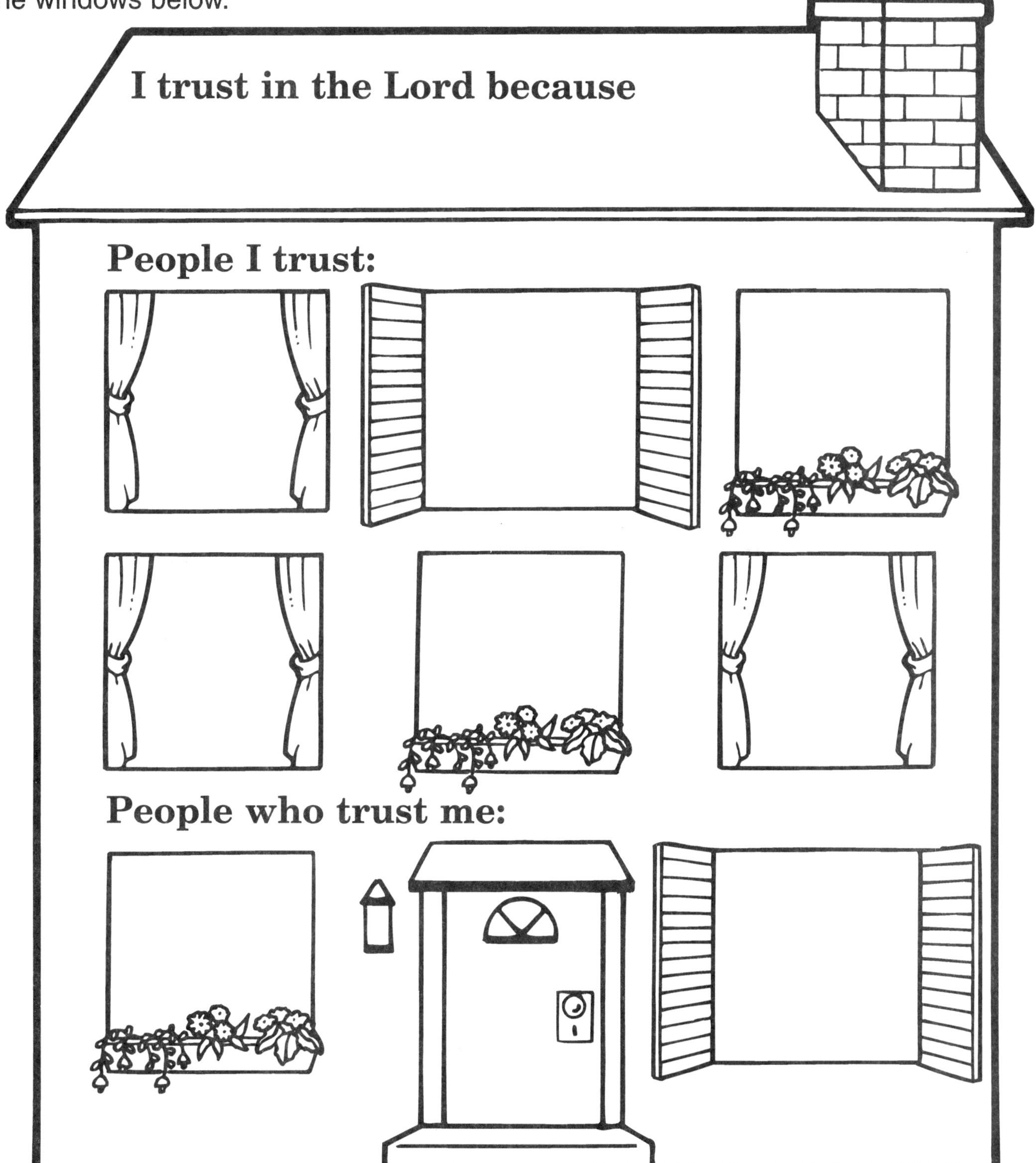

Courage

"... Act with courage, and may the Lord be with those who do well."

2 Chronicles 19:11

SUNDAY	MONDAY	TUESDAY	WEDNESDAY	THURSDAY	FRIDAY	SATURDAY
Write another word for courage.	Draw a picture of you showing courage.	Draw a picture of a time when you needed courage.	Draw a picture of someone from the Bible who needed courage.	Draw a picture of Jesus showing courage.	Design a poster about courage.	Write the word *courage*. Cut out and glue pictures showing courage around it.
Write about a time when you were courageous.	Write a prayer asking God to help others be courageous.	List three courageous people you know.	Create a card for someone who showed courage.	Design an award to give to someone who was courageous.	Write one way Jesus was courageous.	
Read a story about courage. Write the title.	Cut out a picture showing courage. Write about it.	Write a poem about courage. Include the words *strong* and *long*.	Draw a picture of a courageous animal.	List people or things that help you have courage.	Make up a song about courage.	Finish this sentence: *I am courageous when _____.*
Write about a time when you weren't courageous.	Read Deuteronomy 31:6. Memorize the first line. Write it.	Write the definition of courage.		Draw a picture of someone from the Bible who had courage.		Write how your parents are courageous.
Read Daniel 6. Write how Daniel was courageous.	Make a collage of pictures that show courage.		Finish this sentence: *I need courage when _____.*	Write three places where you have shown courage.	Write the name of someone who needs courage.	Write a prayer asking God to help you have courage.

Keep Up Your Courage Booklet

Courage helps you be good and do what is right. You should pray to God for courage.

Below are things courageous people do. Read them and color the pictures if you do these things. Write a sentence about and draw a picture showing courage in each blank box. Then cut out the six boxes. Stack the boxes and staple them on the left side to make a book. Share your book with a friend.

Hope

Put your hope in God, for I will yet praise him, my Savior and my God. *Psalm 42:5–6*

SUNDAY	MONDAY	TUESDAY	WEDNESDAY	THURSDAY	FRIDAY	SATURDAY
Draw a picture of something you hope for yourself.	Write three things for which you hope.	Create a hope collage showing pictures of hope.	Write the definition of hope.	Write why you have hope in God.	Draw a picture showing what you hope God will do for you.	List three things you hope for your parents.
Create a song about hope.	Write a poem about hope.	Write why it is important to have hope.		Design a card to help give a friend hope.	Write three hopes you have for a friend.	Finish this sentence: *Next year, I hope* ___
Draw a picture of you without hope.		Write when you have hope.	List seven things you hope for today.	Write about a hope God probably has for you.	Write three words that rhyme with hope.	Read a story about hope. Write about it.
Cut out a picture showing hope. Write about it.	Finish this sentence: *For my family, I hope* ___	Create a hopeful poster telling others to have hope.		Write about a time you didn't have hope.	Write about a little boy who didn't have hope.	Write what you would tell someone to give him or her hope.
Design a bumper sticker. Write *I Have High Hopes!* on it.	Design a bumper sticker. Write *I Have High Hopes!* on it.	Draw a picture of something you hoped for and got.	Draw a picture of something you hoped for and never got.	Write a prayer asking God to give someone hope.	Draw a picture of an animal. Draw for what it probably hopes.	Write how you hope your day will be today.

GP-75505 Journal Writing Primary

High Hopes

God gives us hope. Hope helps us wish for a lot of things. You can hope that someone sick gets better. You can hope that your Grandma gets the new job she wants. You can even hope that you win your soccer game. Write five things you hope for in the clouds below.

GP-75505 Journal Writing Primary

Family Fun

God sets the lonely in families . . .
Psalm 68:6

SUNDAY	MONDAY	TUESDAY	WEDNESDAY	THURSDAY	FRIDAY	SATURDAY
Draw a picture of you and your family.	Finish this sentence: *I love my family because_______.*	Read Acts 16:34. Write how happy your family is to believe in God.	List three ways your family shows God's love.	Make a collage of things your family likes to do together.	Plan an activity your family can do together.	Draw a picture of something you want your family to do together.
Read Proverbs 31:15. Write how your parents are good parents.	Write a letter telling your family how much you love them.	Write the words *My Family.* Write your family members' names around it.		Draw a picture of Jesus' family.	Write a prayer thanking God for your family.	List four activities your family does together.
	Read a book about families. Write about it.	Write one reason why you love your family.	Draw a picture of a special holiday your family shared.	Write why your family is perfect for you.	Draw a picture of the family you would like to have when you are older.	Write a poem about your family.
List five things families can do together.	Make a special card for each person in your family.	Finish this sentence: *Families are important because __________.*	Write what a family is to you.		Write why you are lucky to have your family.	Plan a perfect vacation for your family.
Draw a picture of where you would like to take your family if you could.	Design a bumper sticker. Write *Families Are Great!* on it.	Draw a picture of someone you would like to add to your family.	Write about a time when you were proud of your family.	Write a prayer praying for people who don't have families.		Write why you think your family is the best.

GP-75505 Journal Writing Primary

A Fantastic Family

Families can have so much fun together. God gave us families so we wouldn't be lonely. He wants us to love and be loved.

Have fun with your family by playing the fantastic Family Fun game on page 30. Color the gameboard. Find a marker for each player. Take turns rolling a die and moving that number of spaces. Do what is asked for on the space. The first family member to the finish is fantastic!

A Time for Us

All families share special times. Draw or glue a picture below of a special time your family shared. Write about it. Cut out the box and display it on your refrigerator.

Our family had a special time when we _________________

____

____

____

____

Family Fun Game

My Fantastic Family Chart

God gave you a wonderful family. It is important to do nice things for the people in your family. It is also important to remember days that are special to them like birthdays and anniversaries.

Use the chart below to record any special days that are important to you and your family. Hang it up for everyone to see to help them remember these special days.

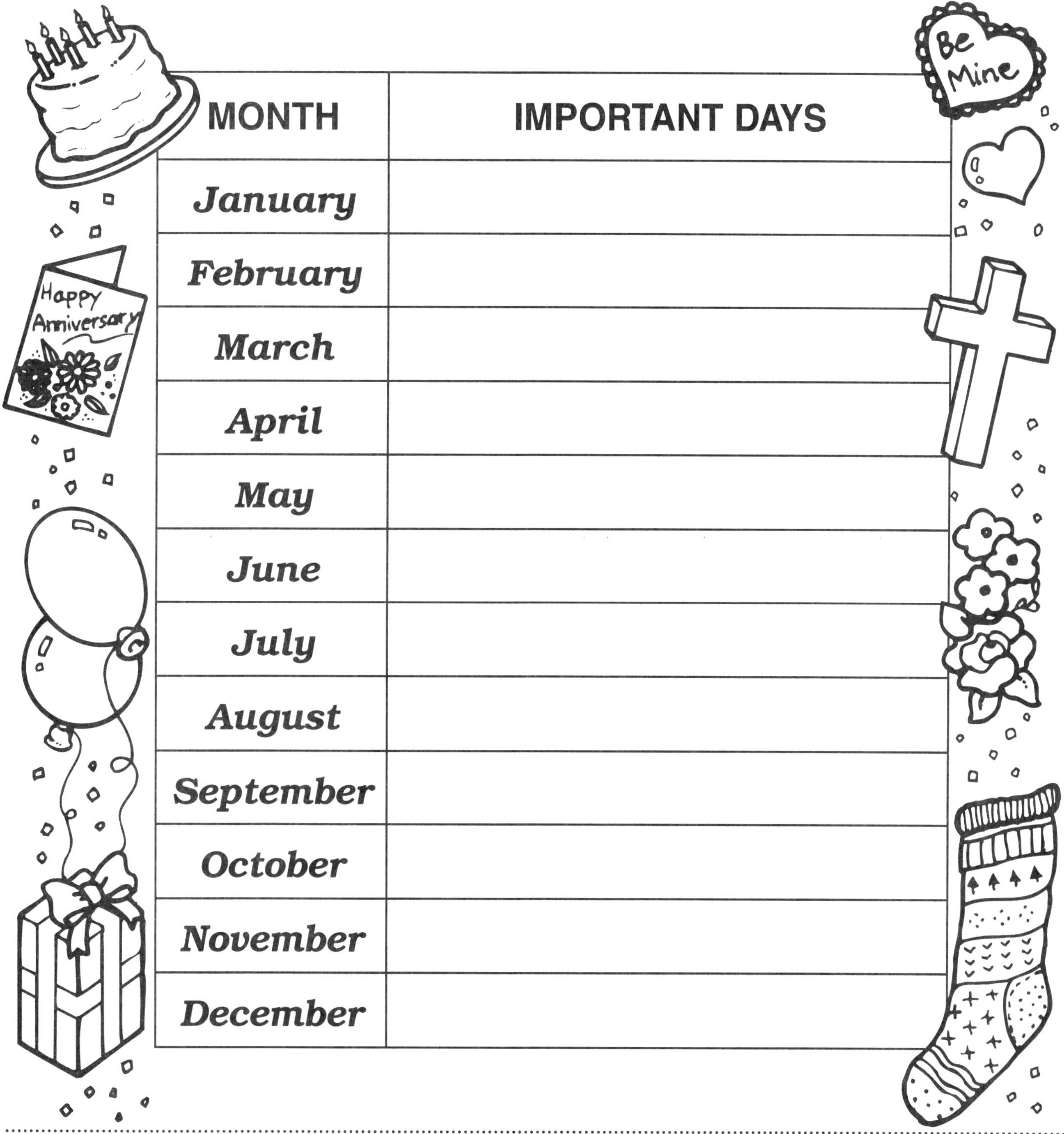

MONTH	IMPORTANT DAYS
January	
February	
March	
April	
May	
June	
July	
August	
September	
October	
November	
December